Inspiration & Wisdom

from the pen of

Henry David Thoreau

Compiled
by
ODELIA FLORIS

Earnest Acorn Books

Grow your reading pleasure

Also by Odelia Floris

Nonfiction:
Inspiration & Wisdom from the Pen of Ralph Waldo Emerson: Over 600 Quotes

Inspiration & Wisdom from the Pen of George Eliot: Over 250 Quotes

Adult fiction:
The Heart of Darkness (The Chaucy Shire Medieval Mysteries Book 1)

The Cockcrow Curse (The Chaucy Shire Medieval Mysteries Book 2)

Beguile Me Not

In Want of a Wife

Rusalka: A Supernatural Czech Fairytale

Children's fiction:
The Little Demon Who Couldn't

www.odeliafloris.com

Contents

"You must live in the present, launch yourself on every wave, find your eternity in each moment. Fools stand on their island of opportunities and look toward another land. There is no other land; there is no other life but this."

"Our life is frittered away by detail. Simplify, simplify."

"Why should we live with such hurry and waste of life?"

"Begin where you are and such as you are, without aiming mainly to become of more worth, and with kindness aforethought, go about doing good."

"The mass of men lead lives of quiet desperation. What is called resignation is confirmed desperation. From the desperate city you go into the desperate country, and have to console yourself with the bravery of minks and muskrats. A stereotyped but unconscious despair is concealed even under what are called the games and amusements of mankind. There is no play in them, for this comes after work. But it is a characteristic of wisdom not to do desperate things."

"I went to the woods because I wished to live deliberately, to front only the essential facts of life, and see if I could not learn what it had to teach, and not, when I came to die, discover that I had not lived. I did not wish to live what was not life, living is so dear; nor did I wish to practice resignation, unless it was quite necessary. I wanted to live deep and suck out all the marrow of life, to live so sturdily and Spartan-like as to put to rout all that was not life, to cut a broad swath and shave close, to drive life into a corner, and reduce it to its lowest terms."

"However mean your life is, meet it and live it; do not shun it and call it hard names. It is not so bad as you are. It looks poorest when you are richest. [...] Love your life, poor as it is. You may perhaps have some pleasant, thrilling, glorious hours, even in a poorhouse. The setting sun is reflected from the windows of the almshouse as brightly as from the rich man's abode; the snow melts before its door as early in the spring. I do not see but a quiet mind may live as contentedly there, and have as cheering thoughts, as in a palace."

"As if you could kill time without injuring eternity."

"Only that day dawns to which we are awake. There is more day to dawn. The sun is but a morning star."

"I do believe in simplicity. It is astonishing as well as sad, how many trivial affairs even the wisest thinks he must attend to in a day; how singular an affair he thinks he must omit. When the mathematician would solve a difficult problem, he first frees the equation of all incumbrances, and reduces it to its simplest terms. So simplify the problem of life, distinguish the necessary and the real. Probe the earth to see where your main roots run. "

"Life in us is like the water in a river."

"If we will be quiet and ready enough, we shall find compensation in every disappointment."

"Renew thyself completely each day."

"The greatest gains and values are farthest from being appreciated. We easily come to doubt if they exist. We soon forget them. They are the highest reality. Perhaps the facts most astounding and most real are never communicated by man to man. The true harvest of my daily life is somewhat as intangible and indescribable as the tints of morning or evening. It is a little star-dust caught, a segment of the rainbow which I have clutched."

"Pursue some path, however narrow and crooked, in which you can walk with love and reverence."

"Every path but your own is the path of fate. Keep on your own track, then."

"I can alter my life by altering my attitude.
He who would have nothing to do with
thorns must never attempt to gather
flowers."

"Simplicity, simplicity, simplicity! I say, let
your affairs be as two or three, and not a
hundred or a thousand; instead of a million
count half a dozen, and keep your accounts
on your thumb nail."

"If a plant cannot live according to its
nature, it dies; and so a man."

"I have no doubt that it is a part of the
destiny of the human race, in its
gradual improvement, to leave off
eating animals, as surely as savage
tribes have left off eating each other
when they came in contact with the
more civilized."

"Rise free from care before the dawn, and
seek adventures."

*"Time is but the stream I go a-fishing
in. I drink at it; but while I drink I see
the sandy bottom and detect how
shallow it is. Its thin current slides
away, but eternity remains."*

"As to conforming outwardly and living
your own life inwardly, I do not think much
of that."

"Be resolutely and faithfully what you are;
be humbly what you aspire to be."

*"It is desirable that a man live in all
respects so simply and preparedly that
if an enemy take the town... he can
walk out the gate empty-handed and
without anxiety."*

"The morning, which is the most memorable season of the day, is the awakening hour. Then there is least somnolence in us; and for an hour, at least, some part of us awakes which slumbers all the rest of the day and night... All memorable events, I should say, transpire in morning time and in a morning atmosphere. The Vedas say, 'All intelligences awake with the morning.'"

"As long as possible live free and uncommitted. It makes but little difference whether you are committed to a farm or the county jail."

"Don't be afraid that your life will end, be afraid that it will never begin!"

"A man sits as many risks as he runs."

"He enjoys true leisure who has time to improve his soul's estate."

"I know of no more encouraging fact than the unquestionable ability of man to elevate his life by conscious endeavor."

"A single gentle rain makes the grass many shades greener. So our prospects brighten on the influx of better thoughts. We should be blessed if we lived in the present always, and took advantage of every accident that befell us, like the grass which confesses the influence of the slightest dew that falls on it; and did not spend our time in atoning for the neglect of past opportunities, which we call doing our duty. We loiter in winter while it is already spring."

"Most men, even in this comparatively free country, through mere ignorance and mistake, are so occupied with the factitious cares and superfluously coarse labors of life that its finer fruits cannot be plucked by them."

"Direct your eye inward, and you will find a
thousand regions in your mind yet
undiscovered. Travel them, and be expert
in home-cosmography."

"I had three pieces of limestone on my
desk, but I was terrified to find that they
required to be dusted daily, when the
furniture of my mind was all undusted still,
and threw them out the window in
disgust."

"Why should we live with such hurry
and waste of life? We are determined
to be starved before we are hungry.
Men say that a stitch in time saves
nine, and so they take a thousand
stitches today to save nine tomorrow."

"If the day and night are such that you
greet them with joy, and life emits a
fragrance like flowers and sweet-scented
herbs, is more elastic, more starry, more
immortal – that is your success."

"Sometimes, in a summer morning, having taken my accustomed bath, I sat in my sunny doorway from sunrise till noon, rapt in a reverie, amidst the pines and hickories and sumaches, in undisturbed solitude and stillness, while the birds sing around or flitted noiseless through the house, until by the sun falling in at my west window, or the noise of some traveler's wagon on the distant highway, I was reminded of the lapse of time. I grew in those seasons like corn in the night, and they were far better than any work of the hands would have been. They were not time subtracted from my life, but so much over and above my usual allowance. I realized what the Orientals mean by contemplation and the forsaking of works. For the most part, I minded not how the hours went. The day advanced as if to light some work of mine; it was morning, and lo, now it is evening, and nothing memorable is accomplished."

"My enemies are worms, cool days, and most of all woodchucks."

"We should go forth on the shortest walk,
perchance, in the spirit of undying
adventure, never to return; prepared to
send back our embalmed hearts only, as
relics to our desolate kingdoms. If you are
ready to leave father and mother, and
brother and sister, and wife and child and
friends, and never see them again; if you
have paid your debts, and made your will,
and settled all your affairs, and are a free
man; then you are ready for a walk."

*"In what concerns you much, do not think that
you have companions: know that you are alone in
the world."*

"My days were not days of the week,
bearing the stamp of any heathen deity,
nor were they minced into hours and
fretted by the ticking of a clock; for I lived
like the Puri Indians, of whom it is said
that 'for yesterday, today, and tomorrow
they have only one word, and they express
the variety of meaning by pointing
backward for yesterday forward for
tomorrow, and overhead for the passing
day.' This was sheer idleness to my fellow-
townsmen, no doubt; but if the birds and
flowers had tried me by their standard, I
should not have been found wanting."

"I think that we may safely trust a good deal more than we do. We may waive just so much care of ourselves as we honestly bestow elsewhere. Nature is well adapted to our weakness as our strength. The incessant anxiety and strain of some is a well nigh incurable form of disease. We are made to exaggerate the importance of what work we do; and yet how much is not done by us! or, what if we had been taken sick? How vigilant we are! determined not to live by faith if we can avoid it; all the day long on the alert, at night we unwillingly say our prayers and commit ourselves to uncertainties. So thoroughly and sincerely are we compelled to live, reverencing our life, and denying the possibility of change. This is the only way, we say; but there are as many ways as there can be drawn radii from one center."

"We must learn to reawaken and keep ourselves awake, not by mechanical aids, but by an infinite expectation of the dawn, which does not forsake us in our soundest sleep."

"Silence is the universal refuge, the sequel to all dull discourses and all foolish acts, a balm to our every chagrin, as welcome after satiety as after disappointment; that background which the painter may not daub, be he master or bungler, and which, however awkward a figure we may have made in the foreground, remains ever our inviolable asylum, where no indignity can assail, no personality can disturb us."

"Be it life or death, we crave only reality. If we are really dying, let us hear the rattle in our throats and feel the cold in the extremities; if we are alive, let us go about our business."

"Every man is tasked to make his life, even in its details, worthy of the contemplation of his most elevated and critical hour."

"The greatest gains and values are farthest from being appreciated. We easily come to doubt if they exist. We soon forget them. They are the highest reality."

"If I should sell both my forenoons and afternoons to society, as most appear to do, I am sure that for me there would be nothing left worth living for. I trust that I shall never thus sell my birthright for a mess of pottage. I wish to suggest that a man may be very industrious, and yet not spend his time well. There is no more fatal blunderer than he who consumes the greater part of his life getting his living."

"We live a short period of time in this world, but we live it according to the laws of eternal life."

"No man ever followed his genius till it misled him. Though the result were bodily weakness, yet perhaps no one can say that the consequences were to be regretted, for these were a life in conformity to higher principles."

"I am convinced, both by faith and experience, that to maintain one's self on this earth is not a hardship but a pastime, if we live simply and wisely."

"Let us spend one day as deliberately as Nature, and not be thrown off the track by every nutshell and mosquito's wing that falls on the rails."

"Read your fate, see what is before you, and walk on into futurity."

"A single footstep will not make a path on the earth, so a single thought will not make a pathway in the mind. To make a deep physical path, we walk again and again. To make a deep mental path, we must think over and over the kind of thoughts we wish to dominate our lives."

"We should be blessed if we lived in the present always, and took advantage of every accident that befell us, like the grass which confesses the influence of the slightest dew that falls on it; and did not spend our time in atoning for the neglect of past opportunities, which we call doing our duty."

"Make the most of your regrets; never smother your sorrow, but tend and cherish it till it comes to have a separate and integral interest. To regret deeply is to live afresh."

"I believe that every man who has ever been earnest to preserve his higher or poetic faculties in the best condition has been particularly inclined to abstain from animal food, and from much food of any kind."

"Happiness is like a butterfly, the more you chase it, the more it will evade you, but if you notice the other things around you, it will gently come and sit on your shoulder."

"We should treat our minds, that is, ourselves, as innocent and ingenuous children, whose guardians we are, and be careful what objects and what subjects we thrust on their attention."

"Follow your genius closely enough, and it will not fail to show you a fresh prospect every hour."

Love and Friendship

"Nothing makes the earth seem so spacious as to have friends at a distance; they make the latitudes and longitudes."

"There is no remedy for love but to love more."

"The language of Friendship is not words, but meanings."

"The most I can do for my friend is simply to be his friend. I have no wealth to bestow on him. If he knows that I am happy in loving him, he will want no other reward. Is not friendship divine in this?"

"Friends... they cherish one another's hopes. They are kind to one another's dreams."

"On the death of a friend, we should consider that the fates through confidence have devolved on us the task of a double living, that we have henceforth to fulfill the promise of our friend's life also, in our own, to the world."

"The heart is forever inexperienced."

"There is danger that we lose sight of what our friend is absolutely, while considering what she is to us alone."

"Man wanted a home, a place for warmth, or comfort, first of physical warmth, then the warmth of the affections."

"A Friend is one who incessantly pays us the compliment of expecting from us all the virtues, and who can appreciate them in us."

"Love must be as much a light as it is a flame."

"We are sometimes made aware of a kindness long passed, and realize that there have been times when our friends' thoughts of us were of so pure and lofty a character that they passed over us like the winds of heaven unnoticed; when they treated us not as what we were, but as what we aspired to be."

"Give me for my friends and neighbors wild men, not tame ones. The wildness of the savage is but a faint symbol of the awful ferity with which good men and lovers meet."

Manners and Speech

"Society is commonly too cheap. We meet at very short intervals, not having had time to acquire any new value for each other. We meet at meals three times a day, and give each other a new taste of that musty old cheese that we are. We have had to agree on a certain set of rules, called etiquette and politeness, to make this frequent meeting tolerable and that we need not come to open war. We meet at the post office, and at the sociable, and at the fireside every night; we live thick and are in each other's way, and stumble over one another, and I think that we thus lose some respect for one another."

"The greatest compliment that was ever paid me was when one asked me what I thought, and attended to my answer."

"A man can suffocate on courtesy."

"There are many fine things we cannot say if we have to shout."

"A perfectly healthy sentence, it is true, is extremely rare. For the most part we miss the hue and fragrance of the thought; as if we could be satisfied with the dews of the morning or evening without their colors, or the heavens without their azure."

"I find it wholesome to be alone the greater part of the time. To be in company, even with the best, is soon wearisome and dissipating. I love to be alone. I never found the companion that was so companionable as solitude."

"If a man does not keep pace with his companions, perhaps it is because he hears a different drummer. Let him step to the music he hears, however measured or far away."

"Things do not change; we change."

"Not till we are lost, in other words not till we have lost the world, do we begin to find ourselves, and realize where we are and the infinite extent of our relations."

"Every generation laughs at the old fashions, but follows religiously the new."

"Could a greater miracle take place than for us to look through each other's eyes for an instant?"

"It is not worth the while to let our imperfections disturb us always."

"My greatest skill has been to want but little."

"I have an immense appetite for solitude, like an infant for sleep, and if I don't get enough for this year, I shall cry all the next."

"I had three chairs in my house; one for solitude, two for friendship, three for society."

"Men have become the tools of their tools."

"Amid a world of noisy, shallow actors it is noble to stand aside and say, 'I will simply be.'"

"See how he cowers and sneaks, how vaguely all the day he fears, not being immortal nor divine, but the slave and prisoner of his own opinion of himself, a fame won by his own deeds. Public opinion is a weak tyrant compared with our own private opinion. What a man thinks of himself, that it is which determines, or rather indicates, his fate."

"We are constantly invited to be what we are."

"It is not that we love to be alone, but that we love to soar, and when we do soar, the company grows thinner and thinner until there is none at all. ...We are not the less to aim at the summits though the multitude does not ascend them."

"In human intercourse the tragedy begins, not when there is misunderstanding about words, but when silence is not understood."

"To be awake is to be alive. I have never yet met a man who was quite awake."

"Enthusiasm is a supernatural serenity."

"The man who goes alone can start today; but he who travels with another must wait until that other is ready, and it may be a long time before they get off."

"He who distinguishes the true savor of his food can never be a glutton; he who does not cannot be otherwise."

"The finest qualities of our nature, like the bloom on fruits, can be preserved only by the most delicate handling. Yet we do not treat ourselves nor one another thus tenderly."

"What people say you cannot do, you try and find that you can."

"Nature is as well adapted to our weakness as to our strength."

"The civilized man is a more experienced and wiser savage."

"We should impart our courage and not our despair."

"The millions are awake enough for physical labor; but only one in a million is awake enough for effective intellectual exertion, only one in a hundred millions to a poetic or divine life."

"There are nowadays professors of philosophy, but not philosophers."

"Some men fish all their lives without knowing it is not really the fish they are after."

"The youth gets together his materials to build a bridge to the moon, or, perchance, a palace or temple on the earth, and, at length, the middle-aged man concludes to build a woodshed with them."

"Humility, like darkness, reveals the heavenly lights."

"To one whose elastic and vigorous thoughts keep pace with the sun, the day is a perpetual morning. It matters not the labors and attitudes of men, morning is when I am awake and there is dawn in me."

"Thus men will lie on their backs, talking about the fall of man, and never make an effort to get up."

"But man's capacities have never been measured; nor are we to judge of what he can do by any precedents, so little have been tried."

"We should come home from far, from adventures, and perils, and discoveries every day, with new experience and character."

"Man is the artificer of his own happiness."

"The better part of the man is soon ploughed into the soil for compost. By a seeming fate, commonly called necessity, they are employed, as it says in an old book, laying up treasures which moth and rust will corrupt and thieves break through and steal. It is a fool's life, as they will find when they get to the end of it, if not before."

"So long as a man is faithful to himself, everything is in his favor, government, society, the very sun, moon, and stars."

"If I knew for a certainty that a man was coming to my house with the conscious design of doing me good, I should run for my life."

"While civilization has been improving our houses, it has not equally improved the men who inhabit them. It has created palaces, but it was not so easy to create noblemen and kings."

"I believe that water is the only drink for a wise man."

"The fate of the country... does not depend on what kind of paper you drop into the ballot-box once a year, but on what kind of man you drop from your chamber into the street every morning."

"Shall a man go and hang himself because he belongs to the race of pygmies, and not be the biggest pygmy that he can? Let everyone mind his own business, and endeavor to be what he was made."

"It is an interesting question how far men would retain their relative rank if they were divested of their clothes."

"The virtues of a superior man are like the wind; the virtues of a common man are like the grass; the grass, when the wind passes over it, bends."

"I believe that the mind can be permanently profaned by the habit of attending to trivial things."

"Men are not so much the keepers of herds as herds are the keepers of men."

"Which is the best man to deal with; he who knows nothing about a subject, and, what is extremely rare, knows that he knows nothing, or he who really knows something about it, but thinks that he knows all?"

"A bore is someone who takes away my solitude and does not give me companionship in return."

"I should not talk so much about myself if there were anybody else whom I knew as well."

"The fault-finder will find faults even in paradise."

Wealth and Charity

"The cost of a thing is the amount of what I will call life which is required to be exchanged for it, immediately or in the long run."

"I would rather sit on a pumpkin, and have it all to myself, than be crowded on a velvet cushion."

"A man is rich in proportion to the number of things which he can afford to let alone."

"That man is the richest whose pleasures are the cheapest."

"Superfluous wealth can buy superfluities
only. Money is not required to buy one
necessary of the soul."

"I am grateful for what I am and have. My
thanksgiving is perpetual. It is surprising
how contented one can be with nothing
definite – only a sense of existence. Well,
anything for variety. I am ready to try this
for the next ten thousand years, and
exhaust it. How sweet to think of! my
extremities well charred, and my
intellectual part too, so that there is no
danger of worm or rot for a long while. My
breath is sweet to me. O how I laugh when
I think of my vague indefinite riches. No
run on my bank can drain it, for my wealth
is not possession but enjoyment."

"The rich man is always sold to the
institution which makes him rich."

"Cultivate poverty like a garden herb, like
sage. Do not trouble yourself much to get
new things, whether clothes or friends."

"I am convinced that if all men were to live as simply as I then did, thieving and robbery would be unknown. These take place only in communities where some have got more than is sufficient while others have not enough."

"Most of the luxuries, and many of the so called comforts of life, are not only indispensable, but positive hinderances to the elevation of mankind. With respect to luxuries and comforts, the wisest have ever lived a more simple and meager life than the poor."

"Spending of the best part of one's life earning money in order to enjoy questionable liberty during the least valuable part of it, reminds me of the Englishman who went to India to make a fortune first, in order that he might return to England and live the life of a poet. He should have gone up garret at once."

"Wealth is the ability to fully experience life."

"Absolutely speaking, the more money,
the less virtue; for money comes between
a man and his objects, and obtains
them for him; it was certainly no great
virtue to obtain it."

"No man ever stood the lower in my
estimation for having a patch in his
clothes: yet I am sure that there is greater
anxiety, commonly, to have fashionable, or
at least clean and unpatched clothes, than
to have a sound conscience."

"None can be an impartial or wise observer
of human life but from the vantage ground
of what we should call voluntary poverty."

"You boast of spending a tenth part of your
income in charity; maybe you should spend
the nine tenths so, and done with it."

"Our houses are such unwieldy property
that we are often imprisoned rather than
housed in them."

"I also have in my mind that seemingly wealthy, but most terribly impoverished class of all, who have accumulated dross, but know not how to use it, or get rid of it, and thus have forged their own golden or silver fetters."

"Philanthropy is... greatly overrated. A pain in the gut is not sympathy for the underprivileged, but the result of eating a green apple; the philanthropist gives to ease his own pain."

Morality and Virtue

"Do not be too moral. You may cheat yourself out of much life so. Aim above morality. Be not simply good, be good for something."

"If you would convince a man that he does wrong, do right. But do not care to convince him. Men will believe what they see. Let them see."

"There are a thousand hacking at the branches of evil to one who is striking at the root."

"We are born as innocents. We are polluted by advice."

"The greater part of what my neighbors call good I believe in my soul to be bad, and if I repent of anything, it is very likely to be my good behavior. What demon possessed me that I behaved so well?"

"Our whole life is startlingly moral. There is never an instant's truce between virtue and vice."

"To be right is more honorable than to be law abiding."

"It is within the soul of the individual that the battle between good and evil is waged and ultimately won or lost."

"While civilization has been improving our houses, it has not equally improved the men who are to inhabit them."

"Goodness is the only investment that never fails."

"The perception of beauty is a moral test."

"Every man is the builder of a temple,
called his body, to the god he worships,
after a style purely his own, nor can he get
off by hammering marble instead. We are
all sculptors and painters, and our material
is our own flesh and blood and bones. Any
nobleness begins at once to refine a man's
features, any meanness or sensuality to
imbrute them."

*"The path of least resistance leads to crooked
rivers and crooked men."*

"I am glad to have drunk water so long, for
the same reason that I prefer the natural
sky to an opium-eater's heaven. I would
fain keep sober always; and there are
infinite degrees of drunkenness. I believe
that water is the only drink for a wise man;
wine is not so noble a liquor; and think of
dashing the hopes of a morning with a cup
of warm coffee, or of an evening with a dish
of tea! Ah, how low I fail when I am
tempted by them! Even music may be
intoxicating. Such apparently slight causes
destroyed Greece and Rome, and will
destroy England and America. Of all
ebriosity, who does not prefer to be
intoxicated by the air he breathes?"

"There is no odor so bad as that which arises from goodness tainted."

"I sat at a table where were rich food and wine in abundance, an obsequious attendance, but sincerity and truth were not; and I went away hungry from the inhospitable board. The hospitality was as cold as the ices."

"Dreams are the touchstones of our characters. We are scarcely less afflicted when we remember some unworthiness in our conduct in a dream, than if it had been actual, and the intensity of our grief, which is our atonement, measures inversely the degree by which this is separated from an actual unworthiness. For in dreams we but act a part which must have been learned and rehearsed in our waking hours, and no doubt could discover some waking consent thereto. If this meanness has not its foundation in us, why are we grieved at it?"

"He is blessed who is assured that the animal is dying out in him every day by day, and the divine being established."

"No humane being, past the thoughtless age of boyhood, will wantonly murder any creature, which holds its life by the same tenure that he does."

"Did ever a man try heroism, magnanimity, truth, sincerity, and find that there was no advantage in them? that it was a vain endeavor?"

Work and Vocation

"A man may be very industrious, and yet not spend his time well. There is no more fatal blunderer than he who consumes the greater part of life getting his living."

"If a man walks in the woods for love of them half of each day, he is in danger of being regarded as a loafer; but if he spends his whole day as a speculator, shearing off those woods and making the earth bald before her time, he is esteemed an industrious and enterprising citizen."

"For it matters not how small the beginning may seem to be: what is once well done is done forever."

"All men want, not something to do with, but something to do, or rather something to be."

"The ways by which you may get money almost without exception lead downward. To have done anything by which you earned money merely is to have been truly idle or worse. If the laborer gets no more than the wages which his employer pays him, he is cheated, he cheats himself. If you would get money as a writer or lecturer, you must be popular, which is to go down perpendicularly. Those services which the community will most readily pay for, it is most disagreeable to render. You are paid for being something less than a man. The State does not commonly reward a genius any more wisely. Even the poet laureate would rather not have to celebrate the accidents of royalty. He must be bribed with a pipe of wine; and perhaps another poet is called away from his muse to gauge that very pipe."

"Do not hire a man who does your work for money, but him who does it for love of it."

"I learned this, at least, by my experiment; that if one advances confidently in the direction of his dreams, and endeavors to live the life which he has imagined, he will meet with a success unexpected in common hours. He will put some things behind, will pass an invisible boundary; new, universal, and more liberal laws will begin to establish themselves around and within him; or the old laws be expanded, and interpreted in his favor in a more liberal sense, and he will live with the license of a higher order of beings. In proportion as he simplifies his life, the laws of the universe will appear less complex, and solitude will not be solitude, nor poverty poverty, nor weakness weakness. If you have built castles in the air, your work need not be lost; that is where they should be. Now put the foundations under them."

"I say, beware of all enterprises that require new clothes, and not rather a new wearer of clothes."

"This world is a place of business. What an infinite bustle! I am awaked almost every night by the panting of the locomotive. It interrupts my dreams. There is no Sabbath. It would be glorious to see mankind at leisure for once. It is nothing but work, work, work. I cannot easily buy a blank-book to write thoughts in; they are commonly ruled for dollars and cents. An Irishman, seeing me making a minute in the fields, took it for granted that I was calculating my wages. If a man was tossed out of a window when an infant, and so made a cripple for life, or scared out of his wits by the Indians, it is regretted chiefly because he was thus incapacitated for – business! I think that there is nothing, not even crime, more opposed to poetry, to philosophy, ay, to life itself, than this incessant business."

"It is not enough to be industrious; so are the ants. What are you industrious about?"

"I desire that there may be as many different persons in the world as possible; but I would have each one be very careful to find out and pursue his own way, and not his father's or his mother's or his neighbor's instead. The youth may build or plant or sail, only let him not be hindered from doing that which he tells me he would like to do."

"Men and boys are learning all kinds of trades but how to make men of themselves. They learn to make houses; but they are not so well housed, they are not so contented in their houses, as the woodchucks in their holes. What is the use of a house if you haven't got a tolerable planet to put it on? – If you cannot tolerate the planet that it is on? Grade the ground first. If a man believes and expects great things of himself, it makes no odds where you put him, or what you show him ... he will be surrounded by grandeur. He is in the condition of a healthy and hungry man, who says to himself, – How sweet this crust is!"

"Our inventions are wont to be pretty toys, which distract our attention from serious things. They are but improved means to an unimproved end, an end which it was already but too easy to arrive at; as railroads lead to Boston or New York. We are in great haste to construct a magnetic telegraph from Maine to Texas; but Maine and Texas, it may be, have nothing important to communicate."

Wisdom and Truth

"Rather than love, than money, than fame, give me truth."

"The question is not what you look at, but what you see."

"To be a philosopher is not merely to have subtle thoughts, nor even to found a school, but so to love wisdom as to live according to its dictates, a life of simplicity, independence, magnanimity and trust."

"Say what you have to say, not what you ought. Any truth is better than make-believe."

"The universe is wider than our views of it."

50

"One farmer says to me, 'You cannot live on vegetable food solely, for it furnishes nothing to make bones with;' and so he religiously devotes a part of his day to supplying his system with the raw material of bones; walking all the while he talks behind his oxen, which, with vegetable-made bones, jerk him and his lumbering plow along in spite of every obstacle."

"What sort of philosophers are we, who know absolutely nothing of the origin and destiny of cats?"

"When we are unhurried and wise, we perceive that only great and worthy things have any permanent and absolute existence, that petty fears and petty pleasures are but the shadow of the reality."

"It is better to have your head in the clouds, and know where you are... than to breathe the clearer atmosphere below them, and think that you are in paradise."

"I have always been regretting that I was not as wise as the day I was born."

"In the morning I bathe my intellect in the stupendous and cosmogonal philosophy of the Bhagvat Geeta, since whose composition years of the gods have elapsed, and in comparison with which our modern world and its literature seem puny and trivial; and I doubt if that philosophy is not to be referred to a previous state of existence, so remote is its sublimity from our conceptions. I lay down the book and go to my well for water, and lo! there I meet the servant of the Bramin, priest of Brahma and Vishnu and Indra, who still sits in his temple on the Ganges reading the Vedas, or dwells at the root of a tree with his crust and water jug. I meet his servant come to draw water for his master, and our buckets as it were grate together in the same well. The pure Walden water is mingled with the sacred water of the Ganges."

"It takes two to speak the truth – one to speak and another to hear."

"Even the best things are not equal to their fame."

"And I am sure that I never read any memorable news in a newspaper. If we read of one man robbed, or murdered, or killed by accident, or one house burned, or one vessel wrecked, or one steamboat blown up, or one cow run over on the Western Railroad, or one mad dog killed, or one lot of grasshoppers in the winter, - we need never read of another. One is enough. If you are acquainted with the principle, what do you care for a myriad instances and applications?"

"All change is a miracle to contemplate, but it is a miracle which is taking place every instant."

"Confucius said, 'To know that we know what we know, and that we do not know what we do not know, that is true knowledge.'"

"We hear and apprehend only what we already half know."

"My desire for knowledge is intermittent; but my desire to bathe my head in atmospheres unknown to my feet is perennial and constant"

"It is never too late to give up our prejudices. No way of thinking or doing, however ancient, can be trusted without proof. What everybody echoes or in silence passes by as true today may turn out to be falsehood tomorrow, mere smoke of opinion, which some had trusted for a cloud that would sprinkle fertilizing rain on their fields."

"It is remarkable how long men will believe in the bottomlessness of a pond without taking the trouble to sound it."

"Truth strikes us from behind and in the dark, as well as from before and in broad daylight."

"Let us settle ourselves, and work and wedge our feet downwards through the mud and slush of opinion and tradition, and pride and prejudice, appearance and delusion, through the alluvium which covers the globe, through poetry and philosophy and religion, through church and state, through Paris and London, through New York and Boston and Concord, till we come to a hard bottom that rocks in place which we can call reality and say, 'This is and no mistake.'"

"The highest that we can attain to is not Knowledge, but Sympathy with Intelligence. I do not know that this higher knowledge amounts to anything more definite than a novel and grand surprise on a sudden revelation of the insufficiency of all that we called Knowledge before, – a discovery that there are more things in heaven and earth than are dreamed of in our philosophy."

"Truths and roses have thorns about them."

"A grain of gold will gild a great surface, but not so much as a grain of wisdom."

"I am sorry to think that you do not get a man's most effective criticism until you provoke him. Severe truth is expressed with some bitterness."

"The light which puts out our eyes is darkness to us."

"Knowledge does not come to us by details, but in flashes of light from heaven."

"The tops of mountains are among the unfinished parts of the globe, whither it is a slight insult to the gods to climb and pry into their secrets, and try their effect on our humanity. Only daring and insolent men, perchance, go there."

"Why level downward to our dullest perception always, and praise that as common sense? The commonest sense is the sense of men asleep, which they express by snoring."

"What is most of our boasted so-called knowledge but a conceit that we know something, which robs us of the advantage of our actual ignorance?"

"All this worldly wisdom was once the unamiable heresy of some wise man."

"As the least drop of wine tinges the whole goblet, so the least particle of truth colors our whole life. It is never isolated, or simply added as treasure to our stock. When any real progress is made, we unlearn and learn anew what we thought we knew before."

"How can a man be satisfied to entertain an opinion merely, and enjoy it?"

"Shams and delusions are esteemed for soundest truths, while reality is fabulous."

"We cannot see anything until we are possessed with the idea of it, take it into our heads, – and then we can hardly see anything else."

"The surface of the earth is soft and impressible by the feet of men; and so with the paths which the mind travels. How worn and dusty, then, must be the highways of the world, how deep the ruts of tradition and conformity!"

"This world is but a canvas to our imaginations."

"The preachers and lecturers deal with men of straw, as they are men of straw themselves. Why, a free-spoken man, of sound lungs, cannot draw a long breath without causing your rotten institutions to come toppling down by the vacuum he makes. Your church is a baby-house made of blocks, and so of the state.

"The church, the state, the school, the magazine, think they are liberal and free! It is the freedom of a prison-yard."

"Any man more right than his neighbors constitutes a majority of one already."

"If the injustice is part of the necessary friction of the machine of government, let it go, let it go: perchance it will wear smooth - certainly the machine will wear out... but if it is of such a nature that it requires you to be the agent of injustice to another, then I say, break the law. Let your life be a counter-friction to stop the machine. What I have to do is to see, at any rate, that I do not lend myself to the wrong which I condemn."

"Unjust laws exist; shall we be content to obey them, or shall we endeavor to amend them, and obey them until we have succeeded, or shall we transgress them at once? Men generally, under such a government as this, think that they ought to wait until they have persuaded the majority to alter them. They think that, if they should resist, the remedy would be worse than the evil. But it is the fault of the government itself that the remedy is worse than the evil. It makes it worse. Why is it not more apt to anticipate and provide for reform? Why does it not cherish its wise minority? Why does it cry and resist before it is hurt? Why does it not encourage its citizens to be on the alert to point out its faults, and do better than it would have them?"

"I heartily accept the motto, 'That government is best which governs least'; and I should like to see it acted up to more rapidly and systematically. Carried out, it finally amounts to this, which also I believe – 'That government is best which governs not at all;' and when men are prepared for it, that will be the kind of government which they will have. Government is at best but an expedient; but most governments are usually, and all governments are sometimes, inexpedient."

"All voting is a sort of gaming, like checkers or backgammon, with a slight moral tinge to it, a playing with right and wrong, with moral questions; and betting naturally accompanies it. The character of the voters is not staked. I cast my vote, perchance, as I think right; but I am not vitally concerned that that right should prevail. I am willing to leave it to the majority. Its obligation, therefore, never exceeds that of expediency."

"There will never be a really free and enlightened state until the state comes to recognize the individual as a higher and independent power, from which all its own power and authority are derived."

"Law never made men a whit more just;
and, by means of their respect for it, even
the well-disposed are daily made the agents
of injustice."

"There are thousands who are in opinion
opposed to slavery and to the war, who yet
in effect do nothing to put an end to them;
who, esteeming themselves children of
Washington and Franklin, sit down with
their hands in their pockets, and say that
they know not what to do, and do nothing."

*"They who have been bred in the school
of politics fail now and always to face
the facts."*

"Must the citizen ever for a moment, or in
the least degree, resign his conscience to
the legislator? Why has every man a
conscience then? I think that we should be
men first, and subjects afterward. It is not
desirable to cultivate a respect for the law,
so much as for the right. The only
obligation which I have a right to assume is
to do at any time what I think right."

"Injustice anywhere is a threat to justice everywhere. We are caught in an inescapable network of mutuality tied in a single garment of destiny. Whatever affects one directly affects all indirectly."

"The government itself, which is only the mode which the people have chosen to execute their will, is equally liable to be abused and perverted before the people can act through it."

"It is not for a man to put himself in such an attitude to society, but to maintain himself in whatever attitude he find himself through obedience to the laws of his being, which will never be one of opposition to a just government, if he should chance to meet with such."

"If any think that their influence would be lost there, and their voices no longer afflict the ear of the State, that they would not be as an enemy within its walls, they do not know how much truth is stronger than errors, nor how much more eloquently and effectively he can combat injustice who has experienced a little in his own person. Cast your whole vote, not a strip of paper merely, but your whole influence."

"Disobedience is the true foundation of liberty. The obedient must be slaves."

"I was not born to be forced. I will breathe after my own fashion. Let us see who is the strongest."

Education

"What does education often do? It makes a straight-cut ditch of a free, meandering brook."

"Though I do not believe that a plant will spring up where no seed has been, I have great faith in a seed. Convince me that you have a seed there, and I am prepared to expect wonders."

"Age is no better, hardly so well, qualified for an instructor as youth, for it has not profited so much as it has lost."

"I mean that they [students] should not play life, or study it merely, while the community supports them at this expensive game, but earnestly live it from beginning to end. How could youths better learn to live than by at once trying the experiment of living? Methinks this would exercise their minds as much as mathematics."

"It's too late to be studying Hebrew; it's more important to understand even the slang of today."

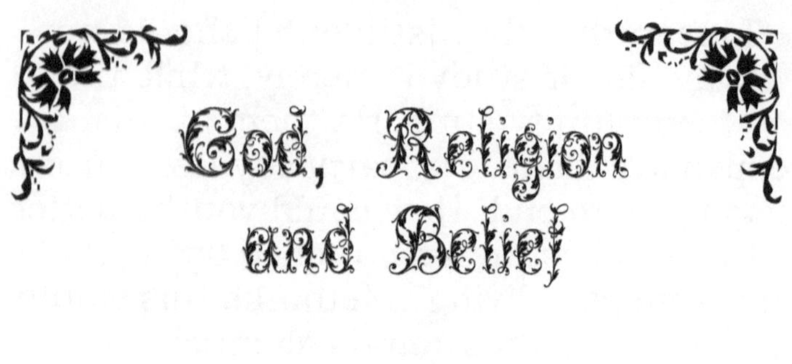

God, Religion and Belief

"I believe in the forest, and in the meadow, and in the night in which the corn grows."

"Heaven is under our feet as well as over our heads."

"I found in myself, and still find, an instinct toward a higher, or, as it is named, spiritual life, as do most men, and another toward a primitive rank and savage one, and I reverence them both. I love the wild not less than the good."

"The church is a sort of hospital for men's souls and as full of quackery as the hospital for their bodies."

"I was once reproved by a minister who was driving a poor beast to some meeting-house horse-sheds among the hills of New Hampshire, because I was bending my steps to a mountain-top on the Sabbath, instead of a church, when I would have gone farther than he to hear a true word spoken on that or any day. He declared that I was 'breaking the Lord's fourth commandment,' and proceeded to enumerate, in a sepulchral tone, the disasters which had befallen him whenever he had done any ordinary work on the Sabbath. He really thought that a god was on the watch to trip up those men who followed any secular work on this day, and did not see that it was the evil conscience of the workers that did it. The country is full of this superstition, so that when one enters a village, the church, not only really but from association, is the ugliest looking building in it, because it is the one in which human nature stoops the lowest and is most disgraced. Certainly, such temples as these shall erelong cease to deform the landscape."

"God is alone, – but the devil, he is far from being alone; he sees a great deal of company; he is legion."

"There are few things more disheartening
and disgusting than when you are walking
the streets of a strange village on the
Sabbath, to hear a preacher shouting like a
boatswain in a gale of wind, and thus
harshly profaning the quiet atmosphere of
the day."

"There is an incessant influx of novelty into
the world, and yet we tolerate incredible
dullness. I need only suggest what kind of
sermons are still listened to in the most
enlightened countries. There are such words
as joy and sorrow, but they are only the
burden of a psalm, sung with a nasal
twang, while we believe in the ordinary and
mean."

"So we saunter toward the Holy Land, till
one day the sun shall shine more brightly
than ever he has done, shall perchance
shine into our minds and hearts, and light
up our whole lives with a great awakening
light, as warm and serene and golden as on
a bankside in autumn."

"We now no longer camp as for a night, but have settled down on earth and forgotten heaven."

"In eternity there is indeed something true and sublime. But all these times and places and occasions are now and here. God himself culminates in the present moment and will never be more divine in the lapse of the ages.'

Art and Literature

"Books are the treasured wealth of the world and the fit inheritance of generations and nations."

"How vain it is to sit down to write when you have not stood up to live."

"When I hear music, I fear no danger. I am invulnerable. I see no foe. I am related to the earliest times, and to the latest."

"Books must be read as deliberately and reservedly as they were written."

"Read not the Times, read the Eternities."

"A taste for the beautiful is most cultivated out of doors"

"We must learn to reawaken and keep ourselves awake, not by mechanical aids, but by an infinite expectation of the dawn, which does not forsake us even in our soundest sleep. I know of no more encouraging fact than the unquestionable ability of man to elevate his life by a conscious endeavor. It is something to be able to paint a particular picture, or to carve a statue, and so to make a few objects beautiful; but it is far more glorious to carve and paint the very atmosphere and medium through which we look, which morally we can do. To affect the quality of the day, that is the highest of arts."

"Read the best books first, or you may not have a chance to read them at all."

"How many a man has dated a new era in his life from the reading of a book."

"The book exists for us perchance which will explain our miracles and reveal new ones. The at present unutterable things we may find somewhere uttered. These same questions that disturb and puzzle and confound us have in their turn occurred to all the wise men; not one has been omitted; and each has answered them, according to his ability, by his words and his life."

"Write while the heat is in you. The writer who postpones the recording of his thoughts uses an iron which has cooled to burn a hole with. He cannot inflame the minds of his audience."

"Readers are plentiful; thinkers are rare"

"To a philosopher all news is gossip, and they who edit and read it are old women over their tea."

"A truly good book... teaches me better than to read it. I must soon lay it down and commence living on its hint. When I read an indifferent book, it seems the best thing I can do, but the inspiring volume hardly leaves me leisure to finish its latter pages. It is slipping out of my fingers while I read... What I began by reading I must finish by acting."

"A written word is the choicest of relics. It is something at once more intimate with us and more universal than any other work of art. It is the work of art nearest to life itself. It may be translated into every language, and not only be read but actually breathed from all human lips; not be represented on canvas or in marble only, but be carved out of the breath of life itself."

"To read well, that is, to read true books in a true spirit, is a noble exercise, and one that will tax the reader more than any exercise which the customs of the day esteem. It requires a training such as the athletes underwent, the steady intention almost of the whole life to this object."

"Books are the treasured wealth of the world and the fit inheritance of generations and nations. Books, the oldest and the best, stand naturally and rightfully on the shelves of every cottage. They have no cause of their own to plead, but while they enlighten and sustain the reader his common sense will not refuse them. Their authors are a natural and irresistible aristocracy in every society, and, more than kings or emperors, exert an influence on mankind."

"If you can speak what you will never hear, if you can write what you will never read, you have done rare things."

"A truly good book is something as natural, and as unexpectedly and unaccountably fair and perfect, as a wild-flower discovered on the prairies of the West or in the jungles of the East. Genius is a light which makes the darkness visible, like the lightning's flash, which perchance shatters the temple of knowledge itself – and not a taper lighted at the hearthstone of the race, which pales before the light of common day."

"If we respected only what is inevitable
and has a right to be, music and poetry
would resound along the streets."

"It has come to this, that the lover of art is
one, and the lover of nature another,
though true art is but the expression of our
love of nature."

"It is not all books that are as dull as their
readers. There are probably words addressed
to our condition exactly, which, if we could
really hear and understand, would be more
salutary than the morning or the spring to
our lives, and possibly put a new aspect on
the face of things for us."

"A sentence should be read as if its author,
had he held a plough instead of a pen,
could have drawn a furrow deep and
straight to the end."

"In books, that which is most generally interesting is what comes home to the most cherished private experience of the greatest number. It is not the book of him who has traveled the farthest over the surface of the globe, but of him who has lived the deepest and been the most at home."

"Men sometimes speak as if the study of the classics would at length make way for more modern and practical studies; but the adventurous student will always study classics, in whatever language they may be written and however ancient they may be. For what are the classics but the noblest recorded thoughts of man? They are the only oracles which are not decayed, and there are such answers to the most modern inquiry in them as Delphi and Dodona never gave. We might as well omit to study Nature because she is old."

"Our moments of inspiration are not
lost though we have no particular poem
to show for them; for those experiences
have left an indelible impression, and
we are ever and anon reminded of
them."

The Natural World

"We need the tonic of wildness... At the same time that we are earnest to explore and learn all things, we require that all things be mysterious and unexplorable, that land and sea be indefinitely wild, unsurveyed and unfathomed by us because unfathomable. We can never have enough of nature."

"Night is certainly more novel and less profane than day."

"Live in each season as it passes; breathe the air, drink the drink, taste the fruit, and resign yourself to the influence of the earth."

"An early-morning walk is a blessing for the whole day."

"Every morning was a cheerful invitation to make my life of equal simplicity, and I may say innocence, with Nature herself."

"Wildness is the preservation of the World."

"A lake is a landscape's most beautiful and expressive feature. It is Earth's eye; looking into which the beholder measures the depth of his own nature."

"Thank God men cannot fly, and lay waste the sky as well as the earth."

"I have a room all to myself; it is nature."

"The keeping of bees is like the direction of sunbeams."

"The squirrel that you kill in jest, dies in earnest."

"He who hears the rippling of rivers in these degenerate days will not utterly despair."

"When I consider that the nobler animal
have been exterminated here – the cougar,
the panther, lynx, wolverine, wolf, bear,
moose, deer, the beaver, the turkey and so
forth and so forth, I cannot but feel as if I
lived in a tamed and, as it were,
emasculated country... Is it not a maimed
and imperfect nature I am conversing with?
As if I were to study a tribe of Indians that
had lost all its warriors... I take infinite
pains to know all the phenomena of the
spring, for instance, thinking that I have
here the entire poem, and then, to my
chagrin, I hear that it is but an imperfect
copy that I possess and have read, that my
ancestors have torn out many of the first
leaves and grandest passages, and
mutilated it in many places. I should not
like to think that some demigod had come
before me and picked out some of the best
of the stars. I wish to know an entire
heaven and an entire earth."

"A gun will give you the body, not the bird."

"Every creature is better alive than dead,
men and moose and pine trees, and he who
understands it aright will rather preserve
its life than destroy it."

> "Every blade in the field – Every leaf in the forest – lays down its life in its season as beautifully as it was taken up."

"I once had a sparrow alight upon my shoulder for a moment, while I was hoeing in a village garden, and I felt that I was more distinguished by that circumstance than I should have been by any epaulet I could have worn."

"I am alarmed when it happens that I have walked a mile into the woods bodily, without getting there in spirit."

"I love Nature partly because she is not man, but a retreat from him. None of his institutions control or pervade her. There a different kind of right prevails. In her midst I can be glad with an entire gladness. If this world were all man, I could not stretch myself, I should lose all hope. He is constraint, she is freedom to me. He makes me wish for another world. She makes me content with this."

"I believe that there is a subtle magnetism in Nature, which, if we unconsciously yield to it, will direct us aright."

"I rejoice that there are owls. Let them do the idiotic and maniacal hooting for men. It is a sound admirably suited to swamps and twilight woods which no day illustrates, suggesting a vast and undeveloped nature which men have not recognized. They represent the stark twilight and unsatisfied thoughts which all have. All day the sun has shone on the surface of some savage swamp, where the double spruce stands hung with usnea lichens, and small hawks circulate above, and the chickadee lisps amid the evergreens, and the partridge and rabbit skulk beneath; and now a more dismal and fitting day dawns, and a different race of creatures awakes to express the meaning of Nature there."

"There is just as much beauty visible to us in the landscape as we are prepared to appreciate, and not a grain more. ...A man sees only what concerns him."

"As long as I have the friendship of the seasons life will never be a burden to me."

"You must converse much with the field and the woods if you would imbibe such health into your mind and spirit as you covet for your body."

"I think that I cannot preserve my health and spirits, unless I spend four hours a day at least – and it is commonly more than that – sauntering through the woods and over the hills and fields, absolutely free from all worldly engagements. You may safely say, A penny for your thoughts, or a thousand pounds. When sometimes I am reminded that the mechanics and shopkeepers stay in their shops not only all the forenoon, but all the afternoon too, sitting with crossed legs, so many of them – as if the legs were made to sit upon, and not to stand or walk upon – I think that they deserve some credit for not having all committed suicide long ago."

"The earth I tread on is not a dead inert mass. It is a body – has a spirit – is organic – and fluid to the influence of its spirit – and to whatever particle of the spirit is in me."

"The stars are God's dreams, thoughts remembered in the silence of his night."

"We can never have enough of nature. We must be refreshed by the sight of inexhaustible vigor, vast and titanic features, the sea-coast with its wrecks, the wilderness with its living and its decaying trees, the thunder-cloud, and the rain which lasts three weeks and produces freshets. We need to witness our own limits transgressed, and some life pasturing freely where we never wander."

"The mission of men there seems to be, like so many busy demons, to drive the forest out of the country."

"Why should I feel lonely? Is not our planet in the Milky Way?"

"Talk of mysteries! – Think of our life in nature, – daily to be shown matter, to come in contact with it, – rocks, trees, wind on our cheeks! The solid earth! The actual world! The common sense! Contact! Contact! Who are we? Where are we?"

"This curious world we inhabit is more wonderful than convenient; more beautiful than it is useful; it is more to be admired and enjoyed than used."

Note from the Publisher

If you enjoyed this quote collection, you are sure to enjoy its companion volumes

Inspiration & Wisdom from the Pen of Ralph Waldo Emerson.

This book presents over 600 quotes for wisdom, inspiration, motivation and living by, each one a gem whose beautiful light will illuminate. Broadly arranged by category, they are carefully chosen and attractively laid out. Ralph Waldo Emerson's insightful, wisdom-filled words are as relevant now as they were when written over 150 years ago. If you are looking for profound yet simple maxims to live by, this book will be an invaluable friend and guide.

Over 600 Quotes

Paperback available on Amazon and Barnes and Noble for $7.99 USD

Inspiration & Wisdom from the Pen of George Eliot

With a touch both loving and wise, George Eliot wrote of many things. But it is her unique insight into human character for which she is valued above all. When reading any one of her great literary masterpieces, the reader is arrested from time to time by some sentence, metaphor or paragraph which sheds astonishing new light on a part of ourselves, the world, or the human condition. We stop, reread it, ponder on its genius and beauty. It is these gems which have been gathered from the great breadth of Eliot's work and are here presented in one concise book. Words on love, marriage, friendship, life, character, virtue, and many more topics, fill these pages. Few will close it without picking up some new pearls to add to their store of wisdom.

Over 250 Quotes

Paperback available on Amazon and Barnes and Noble for $7.99 USD

The Complete Poems of Ralph Waldo Emerson

This book is available on Amazon in paperback for just $13.99 USD.

And lastly, please take a few minutes to leave a brief review of *Inspiration & Wisdom from the Pen of Henry David Thoreau* on Amazon. Authors and publishers are always extremely grateful to receive them. Earnest Acorn Books would love to have yours!